Route 66

▪ MAIN STREET OF AMERICA ▪

BY JUDDI MORRIS

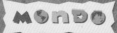

DEDICATION

For Chris and Zoe.

And warm thanks to my editor, Susan Eddy, who told me the book would be cool! You can't beat that. —J.M.

FOR INFORMATION CONTACT

MONDO Publishing
980 Avenue of the Americas
New York, NY 10018

Visit our website at www.mondopub.com

Printed in China

09 10 11 12   9 8 7 6 5 4 3 2

ISBN 1-59336-716-3

COVER AND BOOK DESIGN by Michelle Farinella

PHOTO CREDITS Cover, 2, 6–7, 39, 41, 53: ©Getty Images. 5: ©Hampton Inns. 8, 25: ©Underwood Archives. 9, 11, 15, 28, 33, 36: ©Brown Brothers. 12: ©Marian Clark, The Route 66 Cookbook. 14: ©Underwood &Underwood/CORBIS. 17: Canadian County Historical Museum. 19, 20, 30, 34: ©Bettman/CORBIS: 22, 27: Library of Congress. 23, 38: AP Wide World. 29: ©NHR66F. 37, 43, 46, 47, 49, 50: www.66postcards.com. 41: ©Time & Life/Getty. 44: ©Swa Frantzen. 45: ©Smith Southwestern. 48: ©University of Louisville Photo Archive. 51: ©Lake County Discovery Museum. 52: Wolfgang Kaehler/CORBIS. 57: ©Joseph Sohm/CORBIS. 58: Douglas Kirkland/CORBIS.

Library of Congress Cataloging-in-Publication Data

Morris, Juddi.
  Route 66 : main street of America / by Juddi Morris.-- 1st ed.
    p. cm.
  Includes bibliographical references and index.
  ISBN 1-59336-716-3 (pbk)
 1. United States Highway 66--History--Juvenile literature.
 2. Automobile travel--United States--History--Juvenile literature. I. Title: Route Sixty-six. II. Title.
  HE356.U55M67 2006
  388.1'0973--dc22
          2005016857

CONTENTS

THE MAP OF ROUTE 66

Los Angeles

CALIFORNIA

Songs have been sung and stories and books written about Route 66. In his book *The Grapes of Wrath*, John Steinbeck called this ribbon of asphalt and concrete the "Mother Road." Since it incorporated the main street of each town along its path, Route 66 was also called the "Main Street of America."

Introducing the Mother Road

From the Roaring Twenties until the 1960s, Route 66 was the main highway from the Midwest to the West Coast. The road began in Chicago and ended on a bluff high above the Pacific Ocean in Santa Monica, California. This two-lane highway crossed two-thirds of the nation and rambled through eight states and three time zones.

Traveling Route 66, families might sleep in a wigwam and eat breakfast in a cafe shaped like a shoe or a jackrabbit. They could picnic in the shade of a huge papier-mâché dinosaur and read funny Burma-Shave™ signs along the roadsides.

6

Route 66 was the route taken by thousands of destitute families fleeing the Dust Bowl of the

Middle West in the 1930s. Then, during World War II, troop and supply convoys traveled "66"

to the West Coast. It was also the most popular route ever taken by hordes of tourists,

crisscrossing the United States.

The road was so famed that it had its own television series in the 1960s! The popular series

was based on the travels of two young dudes barreling along Route 66 in a shiny Corvette

convertible. Families ate supper early the night it was broadcast so that parents and kids could

hunker down to watch Tod and Buz streaking along Route 66 to adventure.

This book is about the road west and the most famous highway in America, before

"superslabs" and "progress" passed it by. Much of the social history of our country is

reflected in the rearview mirror of this corridor that stretched almost across the United States.

I love a road of romance,

That speaks of mighty men,

A road that leads me somewhere,

And then back home again.

John Randolph

THE BIRTH OF THE ROAD

The first roads were made by animals that were moving from feeding grounds to watering holes. Early humans followed these paths to hunt the animals. Later, people blazed their own trails, looking for food, water, and fuel. And in time, explorers used those paths as they discovered new lands.

As nations formed, roads were a necessary means of communication and transportation. This was true as early as the reign of Julius Caesar, (49–44 B.C.) when it was said that "all roads lead to Rome." The Romans built more than 50,000 miles (80,465 kilometers) of roads, and some of them are still in use.

All Roads Lead to Rome

Julius Caesar hung a large map on one of the walls of his palace. Made of hammered gold, the map showed the entire road system of Rome. The empire's principal cities were marked by precious emeralds and rubies.

By the time Columbus discovered America, he found Native Americans making crude roads by bending young trees to mark trails. The misshapen trees showed fresh water sources—the branches pointed toward springs and other bodies of water. Later, in colonial Maryland, roads were indicated by notches cut into trees. Two notches marked roads leading to courthouses and churches. Three notches signaled a road leading to a ferry.

But with the coming of the railroad, the public lost interest in road building. Why bother with highways when trains were a cheap way to cross the country? Road building declined, and people traveled mostly where trains could take them.

After the Civil War, however, interest in road building picked up again because of a fabulous invention called the bicycle, which became a popular way to travel. Still, pedaling along rough, tooth-jarring thoroughfares was not much fun. A trip on the two-wheeled contraption usually turned into an endurance test for both rider and vehicle. After pedaling a bicycle along rutted roads, many travelers swore to "get a horse" the next time. They claimed it was easier on the backside because the saddle was bigger and more comfortable.

This curved-dash Oldsmobile runabout was built in about 1901 and cost $650 at the time.

Before long the bicycle took a back seat as a form of transportation. In 1893, the first automobiles were built in the United States. With the arrival of the "horseless carriage" came a clamor for better roads. Drivers wanted places to drive these snorting, smoking little vehicles!

In those days, roads usually followed historic trails. Motorists who ventured onto the Albert Pike, the Ozark Trail, the Santa Fe Trail, or the Old Wire Road were in for hours or even days of adventure, whether they wanted it or not. In 1901, it took six bone-rattling days to go from Kokomo, Indiana, to New York City, a distance of some 700 miles (1,127 km).

The Old Wire Road was one of the most heavily traveled of those roads. It meandered from Joplin to St. Louis, Missouri, and was little more than a beaten path. Horse-drawn carriages, lumbering delivery wagons, and other animal-drawn conveyances, as well as bicycles, traveled its winding length.

Fifth Graders Get Their Kicks on Route 66

Several years ago, a fifth-grade class at William McGinn School in New Jersey took a six-month computerized stationary bicycle trip on Route 66. The students wanted to discover the highway's importance in American culture and history.

They rode westward 20 miles a day, using the Internet to keep in touch with schools, businesses, and people who live and work along Route 66. The students also cooked famous dishes from cafes, diners, and truck stops that tourists once ordered while traveling the Main Street of America.

Their teacher, Anthony Arno, enjoyed the imaginary trip so much that the next summer he took a real bicycle and toured Route 66 from Chicago to Meramec Caverns—a total of about 400 miles (644 km).

Bucketing along such a road was filled with perils. Jagged rocks punctured bicycle or car tires every few miles. When it rained, the road was churned into a mud bog. In a frenzy to keep automobiles churning along, car axles snapped, radiators boiled over, and engines blew up. Not only that—these early automobiles had hand-operated windshield wipers!

Michael Burns, who was a young boy then, told of working in his father's service station in Springfield, Illinois:

> One day there were two fellows who came in here and asked if this was Springfield. I said, "Yes," and they told me to go ahead and service their car. When I told them it came to fourteen gallons of gas and two gallons of heavy oil, they were stunned. "My golly!" they said. "We left home this morning and we was only forty or fifty miles from Springfield." They had turned wrong and had come to Springfield, Illinois, instead of Springfield, Missouri.

A mistake like this was common, since roads were seldom or poorly marked. If a motorist didn't get lost and kept his automobile chugging along, there were few places to buy gas. (A full gas tank in those early vehicles provided about 70 miles (113 km) of travel.) Gasoline was sold by the bucketful and funneled into a car's gas tank.

Although breakdowns, blown tires, and mechanical trouble were common, there were few repair shops outside of towns and cities. Motorists were forced to carry a staggering load of extra motor parts, cans of oil and gas, spare tires, and tire patches. A driver who couldn't fix his own machine might just as well leave it in the barn or stay close to the local repair shop.

A dapper driver tries to reinflate the flat tire on his Ford while his bonneted passenger waits patiently.

On overnight trips, camping gear had to be strapped on the roof, since there were no hotels outside of towns. Taking an automobile trip during this time was more like venturing off on an African safari or a polar expedition.

Then, in 1908, Henry Ford built the Model T Ford and made history. America's love affair with the plucky little automobile began immediately. Although the car did not have a self-starter and had to be cranked by hand, it became a workhorse that would go almost anywhere. Customers could buy the "T" as a two-seater, a sedan, or in various truck models.

Henry Ford Talks About the Model T

"I will build a motorcar for the great multitude. It will be large enough for the family, but small enough for the individual to run and care for. It will be constructed of the best materials, by the best men to be hired, after the simplest designs that modern engineering can devise. But it will be so low in price that no man making a good salary will be unable to own one and enjoy with his family the blessing of hours of pleasure in God's great open spaces."

CHAPTER ONE

The popular Avery's Corner restaurant and service station was 6 miles east of Tulsa, Oklahoma.

By 1926, having mastered the art of mass production, Ford dropped the price of his automobiles. Now more people could buy cars, slide behind the wheel, and hit the open road. These automobile owners, restless to travel, barraged Congress to establish a connected system of interstate highways.

One of the strongest boosters of a cross-country highway was Cyrus S. Avery, who has been called the "Father of Route 66." Avery was determined to see good roads stretch across the nation. "Motor-vehicle traffic does not stop at county lines," he insisted. "Neither does it stop at state lines. America's roads must forsake their provincial, farm-to-market orientation and assume a truly national character."

Avery was appointed Oklahoma State Highway Commissioner and later became a member of the important Associated Highways of America. He was also a consulting highway specialist. This post called for the Oklahoman to map and create a highway system. He and his highway board studied existing trails and roads to see which would be feasible for a federal highway system. Because Avery lived in Oklahoma, he favored a Chicago-to-Los Angeles

Hot Biscuits and Butter

No wonder Cyrus Avery was called the Father of Route 66. He grew up at the intersection of three highways. Cyrus's parents ran a restaurant outside Tulsa, Oklahoma. The red-roofed eatery was famous for its tasty golden-fried chicken, hot biscuits with butter, chocolate cake with thick chocolate icing, and delicious homemade pies. Avery's Corner was one of the most popular restaurants in the state.

ROUTE 66 MAIN STREET OF AMERICA

route, which would travel through a big chunk of his state.

At that time, private road clubs had already marked at least 250 trails throughout the United States. Members of these road clubs lobbied for their stretches of road to be included in the new system. Fierce squabbling broke out, but Avery and his board bowed to nobody. The highway would go through Oklahoma, they said—and it did.

Unlike other highways established at this time, Route 66 did not follow a linear course. It wound out of Chicago and crossed the dark, fertile farmland of Illinois into Missouri. In the "Show Me" state, it tracked the Osage Indian Trail and the Old Wire Road in a southwesterly direction. From there, it followed the Kansas prairie for a way and then plunged into the ranchland and oil fields of Oklahoma and Texas. Then it wound through New Mexico and Arizona, and finally plunged into California, stopping when it reached a bluff above the Pacific Ocean at Santa Monica.

After many battles and standoffs, the route through Oklahoma was accepted on November 11, 1926. In a jubilant mood, Avery wrote to the head of the Division of Design for the Bureau of Public Roads: "We assure you that U.S.66 will be a road through Oklahoma that the U.S. Government will be proud of."

Cyrus Avery, 1927
"The Father of Route 66"

Cyrus Avery, "Father of Route 66," pushed hard to have the road pass through his home state of Oklahoma. He knew that it would help the state economically.

CHAPTER ONE

The Bunion Derby was
one of the most heroic,
if one of the most absurd,
athletic contests ever held.

Anonymous

THE BUNION DERBY ROAD

By 1926, Route 66 was open. Now it was time to let people know that the shortest route from Chicago to the West Coast was ready for travel. Press releases plastered newspaper headlines across the nation, but the best advertising promotion came from a high-rolling promoter named C.C. Pyle. (Some folks said that those initials, C.C., stood for either Cash and Carry or Cold Cash, depending on the audience he was pitching.)

"Why don't we stage the longest foot race in history?" Pyle asked highway officials. Contestants could start in Los Angeles, run through the towns on Route 66 to Chicago, and continue to Madison Square Garden in New York City for a gala celebration. Pyle suggested an entry fee of $100 and a prize of $25,000 for the winner.

This would be no 26-mile marathon, but a serious 3,422-mile

Charles C. Pyle was a born promoter. He is shown here between "Red" Grange, a pro football player, and Suzanne Lenglen, a French tennis star, in about 1926.

(5,507 km) race to the finish! The publicity was sure to benefit Route 66, Pyle insisted. He also promised that towns along the route that chose to feed and offer overnight accommodation to the runners would sell "everything from mousetraps to grand pianos" and become "world famous." Pyle also planned to get rich and world famous himself through endorsements from the manufacturers of shoes, socks, lotions, foot powders, and ointments for sore feet and legs. The National Highway 66 Association gave Pyle's proposal the go-ahead. They thought this was a dandy way to let people know the road was open for travel.

A brother-and-sister marathon dance team hang on in the early 1930s

A race such as the one staged by Pyle did not seem strange at all during the Roaring Twenties. Many promoters seemed to have a gimmick to publicize, and the public loved the resulting excitement. Shipwreck Kelly captured the nation's attention by setting the record for sitting on top of a flagpole (23 days and 7 hours). A craze for marathon dancing was sweeping the country. Couples hit the floor and danced until they dropped. The nation went crazy for teddy bears, and even adults carried them around. Bizarre stunts like live goldfish swallowing became a fad with college students.

Pyle made all the arrangements for the Great Transcontinental Foot Race. On March 4, 1928, a huge crowd of spectators showed up in Los Angeles to watch the 275 runners start the race. Red Grange, a famous football player nicknamed the "Galloping Ghost," gave the countdown and then set off the starting bomb. The contestants took off at a lope on the first leg of the big race.

Among the competitors were some Native Americans who were excellent long-distance

CHAPTER **TWO**

runners. Other entrants included popular athletes and runners from around the United States and throughout the world. But there was also a man toting a ukulele and leading two hound dogs, an old man who walked with a cane, a 15-year-old boy, and an out-of-work actor who leapt across the starting line in a long white robe. Folks ran in bibbed overalls, and suits and ties. Some were barefoot or wore tennis shoes, and others clumped along in boots.

A fascinated audience straggled down the road with the contestants. Many of the athletes' wives, children, and dogs tagged along. There was a press bus, Pyle's private bus, and a hospital van, as well as a food truck and the vehicles of folks who were just along for a lark. A portable radio station and a mock-up of a 3,000-gallon Maxwell House™ coffee pot on a truck added to the weird-looking entourage.

Charles Hart, a 63-year old marathon runner from England, set the pace the first day. By the second day, reporters were calling the race "the Bunion Derby," a term that caught the public's fancy. Already, 77 contestants had dropped out with sore feet. The remaining entrants began pacing themselves for the long haul to Madison Square Garden, several thousand miles away.

The runners were welcomed as heroes in most of the small towns along Route 66. Bands serenaded them, and local citizens held parades in their honor. At night, shows and carnivals entertained the runners. One evening, the folks in a little town staged a show starring a wrestling bear, a tattoo artist, a five-legged pig, a one-legged chicken, a fire-eater, and the mummified body of a real Oklahoma outlaw!

Each day, newspapers, radio announcers, and movie newsreels reported the progress of the contestants, cheered the front-runners, and gave the names of the dropouts. Most runners covered around 40 miles (64 km) a day.

On the darker side, a car hit at least one of the competitors, and others became sick. A few suffered from fallen arches or blisters so bad that they limped off to catch a ride back home. Others just plain quit.

Somewhere along the way, the food concessionaire left. Then the bank foreclosed on Pyle's bus and snatched it, leaving him to beg a ride with members of the press corps. By the next day, however, the vehicle was back on the road, and Pyle claimed the whole thing was "just a terrible mistake" on the part of his creditors.

C. C. Pyle's bus, the "America"

By the time they reached the blazing inferno of the Mojave Desert, almost half of the sunburned runners had given up the grueling race. Route 66 was taking its toll. A weary Pyle, who was not even walking, half-jokingly told people that the letters C.C. in his name stood for Corns and Calluses. Day after day the remaining footsore contestants wearily made their way east. When they reached the Texas Panhandle, a South African and two Finns were leading the pack. Then, just when it looked as if an American would not win, a part-Cherokee farm boy from northeastern Oklahoma struggled to the front of the pack. Wearing the number 43 on his jersey, Andrew Hartley Payne, barely 20 years old, muscled into the lead.

Andy hoped to pay off the mortgage on his family's farm if he won the prize money. When he first considered entering the race, he had asked

Nothing but the Best for C.C. Pyle

C.C. Pyle's bus was the latest thing in road luxury! Built by Fageol Motors, the vehicle cost a cool $25,000 (about $266,606 in today's money). At a time when most Americans didn't even have indoor plumbing, this whale of the road boasted mahogany paneling, hot and cold running water, and a galley with a refrigerator and a gas stove. It sported the best available heating and air conditioning. The bus even had an upper deck with a collapsible awning, where Pyle and his guests loafed in the shade.

CHAPTER **TWO**

the Chamber of Commerce in his hometown of Claremore, Oklahoma, to sponsor him. They discouraged him, saying that he didn't stand a chance. But now that Andy was in the lead, his hometown was plenty proud to claim him.

Although he was the crowd favorite, experts warned people not to get their hopes up. After all, they cautioned, this was Andy's first race. What they didn't know was that the young lad had trained long and hard, running up and down the rolling hills and pastures of his family's heavily mortgaged farm. He wasn't about to lose. Besides, Andy had been in good shape most of his life due to hard physical labor. There was another reason, too. His brothers and sisters rode horseback to school, but Andy, who hated horses, ran to school, and usually beat the riders to the schoolhouse door.

When the contestants reached Oklahoma, crowds lined the streets to see their hero. Schools closed so that students could yell encouragement to Andy. The governor of Oklahoma met him with a motorcycle escort, and mayors tossed him the keys to Oklahoma towns along the way.

Andy's Mom

Andy Payne's mom worried about him the whole time he was running the Bunion Derby. When she finally heard he had won the race, she was so relieved that she fainted! Mrs. Payne was a humble woman, and when she came to, she said that she "hoped the victory wouldn't make Andy big-headed."

Mile after agonizing mile Andy ran, trotted, and walked—often neck-and-neck with a marathoner from England. By the time they reached the outskirts of Claremore, Oklahoma, the contestants had crossed half the United States.

Then, somewhere in the Midwest, Andy got lucky. His main opponent was sidelined with an infected tooth and had to leave the race. From then on, it was Andrew Hartley Payne all the way! Eighty-four consecutive days after leaving Los Angeles, he finished the race hours ahead of the competition. He had run through sandstorms and snowstorms, rain and hail, the blistering

ROUTE 66 MAIN STREET OF AMERICA

hot desert and heavy city traffic. Later, 54 other men staggered across the finish line. Fifty-five contestants had completed the coast-to-coast endurance test, but young Andy Payne had won the race.

Pyle had promised to pay Andy's prize money the day after the contestant's arrival in New York City. The hero arrived May 26, 1928, but there was no ceremony and no money the next day. Rather than getting rich, Pyle had lost around $60,000 on the race. He had to arrange a loan to pay Andy, and he did not get the money together until June 1. When the young Oklahoman finally stepped up to receive his prize money, Pyle handed him not a check but two promissary notes, one to be paid on June 4 and the other on September 4. Months would pass before Andy received all his money, but true to his promise, as soon as he received it, Andy paid off the family farm and even bought more land for his parents.

The Bunion Derby had served its purpose. Americans could hardly wait to travel the new road. They were eager to cross the broad Mississippi River and motor west to see the sights previewed on movie newsreels during the race. But the timing was off. Times were hard. Travel was impossible when just keeping food on the table was becoming a problem. Folks "made do" and stayed at home. They wore their old clothes and bought only the necessities. An ill wind was rising—a wind that would drive thousands of people off their land and onto the road, but not for pleasure driving.

Andy Payne reaching Joliet, Illinois, en route to victory

The Dancing Cowboy

After the Bunion Derby, Andy Payne tried to break into Hollywood show business, calling himself "the Dancing Cowboy from Oklahoma." He didn't have much luck though, and soon enrolled in the University of Arkansas. Eventually Andy returned to Oklahoma. He hung up his running shoes and cowboy duds and became clerk of the Oklahoma Supreme Court and one of the most respected men in his state. When Andy was an old man, someone asked him if he thought such a race as the Bunion Derby could ever happen again. Andy replied, "Nope, today some fool would run me down in his car."

" . . . I'm a goin' down
that road with
troubles on my mind…."

Woody Guthrie

THE DUST BOWL ROAD

The Great Depression was the worst economic disaster the United States had ever faced. Ruined stockbrokers jumped to their deaths from Wall Street windows. Banks failed, and factories closed. Unemployment ranged from about 14 to 25 percent.

Bankrupt businessmen hunched down on street corners, selling apples for a nickel apiece or pencils for a penny. People roamed the streets looking for work, only to be met by signs that said NO HELP WANTED, KEEP OUT. Hungry people lined up for food at free soup kitchens or stood in bread lines for handouts.

Rural America was even harder hit. Farmers had been losing money before the Great Depression began. Foreclosures were forcing many growers off the land. In southwestern

This soup kitchen in Chicago, Illinois, fed about 3,500 people three meals a day during the Depression.

Kansas, southeastern Colorado, northeastern New Mexico, and the panhandles of Texas and Oklahoma, things were even more desperate. Until World War I, this had been cattle-raising country. Then the soaring price of grain encouraged farmers to plow up the grassland and plant wheat. In good years, the light, sandy soil yielded heavy crops. As greater demands for grain continued, horses and mules gave way to tractors and harvesters on Texas-sized spreads.

Because most small farmers did not have money to buy the large equipment needed to compete with big landowners, they lost their land and became tenants or migrant workers on the same large farms that had squeezed them out. The Great Plains also faced an overwhelming drought from 1933 to 1937 that turned the area into a giant bowl of dust.

Farmers had mistreated this land for years. They had plowed and planted the same crops season after season with no thought of conserving the land. Now, there was little topsoil left. Less than 50 years after Oklahoma had become a state, much of its land was drained of nutrients. When the wind began to blow over the worn-out land, the light soil rose into the air. Dust storms, 2 or more miles high and 200 miles (322 km) wide, traveling as fast as 50 miles (80 km) an hour, laid waste to the countryside. Houses and barns were banked with sand, and roads and fences were covered. Planted crops were smothered with dirt and died. Dunes as high as 30 feet (9 m) piled up. Oklahoma alone experienced up to 352 dust storms during this time.

Still, no rain fell, and the dust storms continued. Day turned to night during those "black blizzards." People tied wet sacks over their heads, ventured out to care for their livestock, and then

Prices During the 1920s

During the 1920s, the average family wage in the United States was about $100 a month or $1,200 a year. However Henry Ford paid his automobile assembly-line workers $5 a day, or $1,500 a year. A loaf of bread cost 9 cents, utility bills of gas, water, and electricity usually averaged a dollar a month. You could buy a nice house for about $1,000.

CHAPTER **THREE**

A farmer and his sons try to walk in the face of a dust storm in Oklahoma.

Black Day

On May 10, 1934, 300 million tons of topsoil whipped into the air so high the sun was obscured. People were terrorized. Skies remained dark on the East Coast for five hours, and some 12 million tons of plains soil fell on Chicago. A ship 300 miles (483 km) off the coast of New York radioed for an explanation of all the dust in the air!

fled back into their houses. But even with windows and doors barred and covered with blankets and sheets, the dust seeped inside. Finally people covered themselves and their whimpering children with wet blankets and cowered in corners. Even indoors it was hard to breathe. There seemed to be no way to keep the blowing dust out. Many people died of what was called "dust pneumonia."

Some of the dust storms lasted as long as 72 hours. Schools and businesses closed, and cars and trains stopped running. Flocks of wild geese lost their bearings and plummeted to earth. Livestock choked to death or died of thirst. Those that lived had no food; pasture grass was so clogged with dirt that the animals could not eat it.

With no crops to harvest, there was no money. Small shops and businesses that depended on the business of the farm community went broke. Even grocery stores had to refuse people credit, for the owners had no money to pay their suppliers.

People were hungry. They had lost hope. To them, the American dream of making a living on a little piece of land was dead and lay buried in the choking dust. It was then that thousands of people loaded their raggedy possessions and families into their old cars and trucks and headed west. They lit out for Route 66, the road of flight and hope that John Steinbeck wrote about in *The Grapes of Wrath*. Many of the affected areas lost 60 percent of their population. People simply walked away from their homes and farms.

Some didn't even bother to close the doors. There was nothing worth stealing, and dust covered everything.

This mass exodus from the ten Great Plains states was the greatest westward migration ever made. An estimated 210,000 people migrated to California during that time. Since Oklahoma was the worst victim of the dust storms, those who departed the Great Plains were labeled "Okies."

Most had just enough money to buy a tank of gasoline and a little food. But they were pitifully eager to pay their way. They stopped to work on farms, cut wood for householders in small towns, raked yards, washed cars, washed dishes, or hoed weeds. They were willing to work at almost any job to earn enough to get to the next town and on to California, where they hoped to start a new life.

Flossie Haggard, the mother of country-western singer Merle Haggard, tells how her family fled the Dust Bowl:

Country music legend Merle Haggard and his sister donated family belongings taken on their move along Route 66 from Oklahoma to California to the Smithsonian in 2003.

> In July, 1935, we loaded some necessary supplies onto a two-wheel trailer and our 1926 model Chevrolet, which Jim had overhauled. We headed for California on Route 66, as many friends and relatives had already done. We had our groceries with us—home sugar-cured bacon in a lard can, potatoes, canned vegetables, and fruit. We camped at night, and I cooked in a Dutch oven. The only place we didn't sleep out was

23

Like the World Was Blowing Away

Ruby Hicks, who suffered through those dust bowl years in a small town in Oklahoma, shudders as she remembers thick, whirling clouds of dust blowing day after day. "Good heavens, I never saw anything like it and hope I never do again. It would cloud up and get dark like it was going to rain. The thunder rattled and boomed over our heads and the lightning flashes were fierce. You could almost feel it sizzling. But it didn't rain. After all that ruckus it just blew in another dust storm thicker than the last one. Even the trees died. There was nothing to hold the ground. It was like the world was coming to an end."

in Albuquerque, where we took a cabin and where I can remember bathing. When the Haggards reached the desert, their old car broke down.

We were out of water, and just when I thought we weren't going to make it, I saw this boy coming down the highway on a bicycle. He was going all the way from Kentucky to Fresno. He shared a quart of water with us and helped us fix the car. Everybody'd been treating us like trash, and I told this boy, "I'm glad to see there's still some decent folks left in this world."

As streams of dust bowl victims took to the highway, people in towns along the way grew resentful of "those Okies." Most inhabitants of the little communities along Route 66 were barely making a living themselves. They did not want penniless families hanging around, so many gas stations and grocery stores gave these nomads just enough fuel and food to get to the next town. Then the hungry, whimpering children, the broken-spirited men, and their sad-eyed women would become the next location's problem—anything to get these folks and their rattling, bald-tired old vehicles back on "66" and out of their community. Some people even set the law on Okies who looked as if they might stay. As folk singers Woody Guthrie and Pete Seeger sang:

The police in yo town,

They shove me around.

I got them Highway 66 blues.

This family of Okies were four of the approximately 375,000 who fled the dust bowl and headed west in the 1930s.

Of course, there were good Samaritans along Route 66 who helped dust bowl victims and treated them with kindness. These kind-hearted people realized that these sad families were responsible, hard-working people who were just down on their luck.

And so the homeless struggled from town to town, moving toward California, where sweet, juicy oranges grew on trees, and where life would be better. But when they reached the mountains of New Mexico, some turned back in defeat. Near Thoreau, New Mexico, the Continental Divide at 7,275 feet (2,217 m) was the highest point of the highway. It looked insurmountable to these Great Plains people, who had never seen anything higher than a hill. They were afraid to drive the narrow, switchback mountain roads. Usually their old cars and trucks were in such poor condition that they didn't even have the power to ascend the steep elevations. Those with better cars and a little cash paid local people to drive their vehicles over the mountain passes, while the migrating adults and children sat crowded together, white-knuckled and terrified that the brakes would not hold on the downgrade of the steep mountain roads.

The sweet relief they felt after finally putting the mountain ranges behind them did not last long. The burning desert stretched ahead. Never had they experienced such brutal temperatures. Waves of heat shimmered in the distance. Mirages that looked like cool water covering the highway were always just out of reach.

It was at this point, with all hope gone, that others turned back. Most had not known that they had to cross a sizzling wasteland before reaching the ocean, the shade of citrus groves, the grape vineyards, and farms of California. Many who had only heard or read of the Golden State and believed the stories of a land of "milk and honey" now decided that it had been a cruel joke. They were sure the rest of the state looked exactly like the 300 miles (483 km) of desolate land they'd just encountered, and they wanted no part of it. Those who continued were made of the stronger stuff that Woody Guthrie, a dust bowl survivor, sang about:

> Been held down, beat down, shut down, nailed down, set down, drove down, shoved down, chopped down, hoed down, plowed under, held under, dusted under, tractored under, shot at and missed, spit at and hit. But we ain't down yet!

Many travelers, tired and hungry, broke and discouraged, forged through the desert, clawed their way over Cajon Pass, and dropped into the beautiful country and cool weather they had dreamed of for so many miles. But what finally changed the fortunes of many of the migrants who came to California was not the farm work they found—it was World War II. Months before America joined the Allies against Hitler, war had seemed inevitable to President Franklin Roosevelt. He had launched a preparedness program by building defense plants in California. These plants would hire thousands of men and women and pay them good wages.

Oklahoma singer Woody Guthrie hitchhiked, rode freight trains, and even walked to California in the migration of dust bowl refugees.

27

Chapter Four

Those convoys passed
through here night
and day and every
day of the week,
a continuous line
of olive drab vehicles…
traveling 35 miles
an hour, going
to war….

Old-timer from
Barstow, California

THE WORLD WAR II SUPPLY ROAD

December 7, 1941, was a quiet Sunday morning at the U.S. Naval Base at Pearl Harbor, Hawaii, when waves of Japanese aircraft appeared overhead. The planes had taken off from carriers in the Pacific and began pounding the naval base with bombs in a surprise attack.

The next day President Franklin D. Roosevelt announced on the radio that the United States was at war with Japan. On December 11, Germany and Italy declared war on the United States. More than 16 million Allied troops would soon be fighting the major Axis powers of Germany, Italy, and Japan in Europe and the Pacific.

Since the United States had to fight on two fronts, a mighty effort was required. Automobile tires were rationed, and soon automobiles were, too. Gasoline, rubber footwear, and fuel oil for household use were added to a long list of items needed by the military. By 1943,

President Franklin D. Roosevelt signs the Declaration of War against Japan on December 8, 1941.

28

leather footwear, canned fruits and vegetables, meat, and fat were also rationed items.

Civilian automobile owners received a basic ration of gasoline, although doctors, farmers, and other "essential users" were allowed more. Absolutely no gasoline for pleasure driving or traveling was allowed. Without cars, fuel, or tires, tourist travel ground to a halt across the United States. During this time, folks said that you could see more jackrabbits and tumbleweed than cars on Route 66. Until military convoys and troops began to move, times were hard along the road. But soon hordes of people headed to the West Coast to "help win the war." Once more, a mighty migration streamed west on the Mother Road—this time to build ships, airplanes, and other military equipment.

The old Chain of Rocks Bridge, closed in 1967, was reopened in 1999 for bicyclists and pedestrians.

Among those were Lela Bird, her husband, and children, "fruit tramps" who were traveling Route 66, picking cotton in Arizona, harvesting

Cross a Crooked Bridge

Most bridges soar straight across a river. The Chain of Rocks Bridge over the Mississippi between the states of Illinois and Missouri does not. The construction of the span started on the Missouri side, where the engineers set the pilings on bedrock and built the bridge straight out to the middle of the Mississippi River. But builders on the Illinois site could not line up their span of the bridge with the opposite side because there was no suitable bedrock at that location. After two failed attempts to sink pilings, the Illinois engineers moved upriver some 200 yards to try again. They had to point the bridge downstream to meet the other half, which caused the bridge to take a turn in the middle of the river. The speed limit at the turn was 15 miles per hour. The pavement was about 18 feet (5.4 m) wide, and the shoulders were steel girders. The jog in the bridge was a traffic bottleneck, especially when trucks going in opposite directions met there. One would have to wait while the other carefully jacked itself around. Maneuvers like this caused some of the greatest traffic jams in the history of Route 66.

melons in the Imperial Valley, or bringing in the artichokes in the Salinas Valley. Wherever there was a crop to be harvested, they worked—but the life was hard, and they were always short of money.

Once Lela's husband got a steady job in a defense plant, however, their wandering days were over. They stopped following the crops, settled into a nice home, and enrolled their children in school. In a book she later self-published, *When the Birds Migrated*, Lela Bird tells how much better life was after her husband got steady work that didn't end when the crop was harvested.

For farm workers who continued to bring in the crops, it was a different story from depression times. Growers gave workers a warm welcome. Farmers were desperate for help as they tried to feed the nation, the troops, and Allied countries around the world. So many people were working in defense plants or were in military service that agriculture workers were in short supply. Unlike dust bowl times, migrant workers were begged to stay, not ordered to "move on outta here, folks."

Once more, traffic roared along Route 66 as troops, supplies, and equipment rolled across the country. But people who ran gas stations, cafes, and other roadside establishments found that doing business in wartime could be one big headache. Many foods were no longer available, or were rationed. People were issued ration books, with red stamps for meat, canned fish, cheese, and dairy products; and blue stamps for canned vegetables, fruit, and other products. When they ate at restaurants, unless they were military personnel, people were required to give the proper

Food was not the only thing that was rationed during wartime. This gasoline ration card was issued to Isaac Schmidt of New York for his Pontiac.

number and type of ration stamps.

Buying almost anything along Route 66 was complicated, since the government had rationed so many items. When travelers made a purchase, they tore out the required number of stamps from their ration books. After collecting these stamps, merchants had to stick them into another book and then send them to a government rationing board.

Scarcity of goods was not the only problem. Flying schools and training bases were established along Route 66. Thousands of soldiers were stationed in small towns that were not prepared for the huge influx of people. Wives and children followed their servicemen, determined to be with them until their loved ones were sent overseas.

Kingman, Arizona, a small town of around 3,000, was overrun with some 15,000 servicemen after the Army Air Corps established a gunnery school a few miles away. Military families rented any lodgings they could find. Almost every homeowner in town was renting at least one room to a serviceman's family. One old-timer remembered, "You know, people seem to remember the Golden Rule more during hard times like that. Whenever anybody had gas stamps and could go anywhere, they always picked up hitchhiking servicemen. You never saw a car with just one person in it, unless it was the local doctor on his way to make a house call."

Oh, Those Penny Loafers

A woman who attended Barstow High School in California during World War II remembers:

"One day a girl came to school wearing new brown penny loafers. Her father was rumored to buy on the black market [an illegal way of obtaining rationed goods during wartime]. The rest of us kids were wearing old shoes because new ones were just not available in stores. Well, when I saw those shiny leather loafers with the copper pennies stuck in the cute little slots across the instep, I felt like I'd just die if I didn't have a pair! Every time I looked over at those shoes during American History class, I wondered why my parents wouldn't buy on the black market. After all, it was only a pair of shoes. When I came home from school that day, there was a letter from my brother in the army. I worshiped my big brother and had cried for days when he went into the service. In this letter he was making a joke about wearing army shoes that didn't fit. After reading that letter, I never again whined about doing without something silly. I'd just think of my brother, wet and cold, slogging through the mud in Italy, wearing shoes that did not fit, and new loafers seemed very unimportant. I'd have gone barefooted to give him comfortable shoes."

As the military machine spat out men and equipment, Route 66 turned into a convoy road, crawling with jeeps and trucks carrying troops and arms. The small amount of civilian traffic was halted until each military convoy passed. A girl who was a high-school student in New Mexico remembers waiting nearly an hour while a long convoy passed:

My dad owned a feed store and made deliveries to ranches. Since gas was rationed, my 14-year-old sister and I rarely got to go anywhere. When we were out of school, he took us on deliveries. One day, we had no more than turned onto "66" when we were flagged down by a military police. He told us a convoy was coming and we must park on the side of the road until it passed.

He was so polite and looked so handsome in his uniform that my sister and I felt very self-conscious. In a minute the military vehicles started rolling past us. My dad smiled and waved at them, so my sister and I did, too. Most of the soldiers waved and grinned back at us, their teeth white in their tired, dusty faces, and some gave my dad a little salute and a V for Victory sign.

I was rarely serious in those days, but as they passed, I felt sad and scared. These guys looked just like the boys I knew in school or just like my brothers and cousins who were in the service.

They would have to kill people and maybe be killed, I thought. That day, I grew up. We were at war and the young people of our country had to fight it. It didn't seem fair. The next Saturday I went with my mother to the Red Cross office to roll bandages and I learned to knit army sweaters. It was the only way I could think of to help.

And so troops and supply lines droned along Route 66, geared up to fight the second world war in a century. Once more, America was trying to "make the world safe for democracy," as President Woodrow Wilson had promised during World War I. The nation had lost 116,708 troops during that war. Over 407,316 American soldiers would lose their lives in World War II.

A convoy of U.S. Army transport vehicles stretches for miles

"I was walking out this morning,
with rambling on my mind."

Chapter Five

Sara Carter

THE TOURIST HIGH ROAD

Although tourism was heavy after World War II, people had actually been hitting the roads in droves as early as 1910, except for during the two world wars. Tired of being tied to railroad schedules, travelers could now climb behind the wheel of their "tin lizzies" and explore the United States. Roads were poor, but Americans were eager to head into the hinterlands (the remote or less developed parts of a country) to see what the rest of the United States was like.

By 1913 there were some 1,194,000 automobiles on the move. Much of this early automobile travel involved camping, as these "tin can tourists" went out to commune with nature. At the end of a day's drive, they could find free camping spots alongside clear, running streams, in schoolyards, or even in a

A 1914 family outing in the Model T

34

farmer's field (with or without his permission). During this time, an article in *American Motorist* echoed many folks' desire to go gypsying:

> There is a bit of the nomad still remaining in most of us. Not that we want to spend our time trading horses and cooking stew over a smoking fire. We passed that state some time ago and thought we were settling down to civilized living, when along came the automobile and made it so easy for us to get from one place to another that our wanderlust reared its head and would not stay down.

But as more car campers swarmed down the road, "No Camping," "No Trespassing," and "Keep Out!" signs began to appear. A plague of travelers was spoiling the countryside with trash and vandalism. Some thought nothing of opening gates and breaking down fences on private farmland. They left their trash littering the pastures. Others invaded orchards, clambered up trees, and picked fruit without permission—knocking down almost as much as they used. One angry landowner even found a group of campers chopping down one of his shade trees for firewood!

By 1920, with more than 8 million cars crowding the roads and trespassing on private property, something had to be done. Many cities began providing free tourist parks for these auto gypsies. Counties and states followed suit, establishing campsites where regulations were strictly enforced, and private property was protected.

There were less adventuresome travelers who had no desire to camp. They claimed they could see enough nature from their open cars.

Stealing Milk From Bossy

An Illinois farmer, whose place was one-half mile from Route 66, caught a camping family milking one of his dairy cows. The wife was holding the cow still with a rope tied around the animal's neck while her husband burgled the milk. When caught, the pair had already collected nearly a gallon bucket of milk. A little way off, their children were tearing around the farmer's cornfields picking armloads of fresh corn on the cob to roast over a campfire.

Goggles, gauntlets, dusters, and boots were worn by intrepid motorists in the early days of recreational driving, when cars were open and roads were dusty.

However, they needed places to stay. They were not interested in stopping overnight at the railroad hotels used by travelers of the past. These non-campers didn't want to be separated from their cars, as they would have been in the railroad hotels. Besides, motorists usually wore special clothes, such as driving goggles splattered with grease, gauntlets (gloves) that came halfway up to their elbows, and long dusters (lightweight coats) covered with layers of road dust. If it was raining, they were splattered with mud from the road. They did not care to parade through a hotel lobby to register in their travel-stained clothes.

In answer to this new need, tourist courts began opening along Route 66. They usually consisted of a cluster or string of cottages, each containing a bedroom, a bath, and a kitchen, with an adjacent garage for the car. These accommodations were often on the outskirts of town, saving motorists the hassle of downtown traffic after a long day of driving. They were also less expensive than hotels with bellboys and doormen who must be tipped. The family car could be parked right next to the cabin, so that it didn't have to be completely unpacked every night. Unlike hotels, where guests must check out before leaving, motorists could pay the bill the night before and leave early the next morning.

Following World War II, people once more resumed the move west. Now, however, they were again traveling for pleasure. In fact, the renowned architect Frank Lloyd Wright, humorously commenting on the latest westward migration, remarked that the continent was tilting, and

Route 66 was the chute down which everything loose was sliding into southern California.

Servicemen were itching to have a good time. Those who had been stationed in the West were eager to show their families where they had trained. Many of these ex-GIs from the Midwest had come to love the western states. After returning home, they packed up their wives and children and moved back to warmer climates and year-round blue skies.

One such serviceman was 27-year-old Bobby Troup, a young musician who had visited southern California on his way overseas. Bobby had decided that if he lived through the war, he would move from Harrisburg, Pennsylvania, to Hollywood the moment he got out of the service. Troup had already written one hit tune and hoped to make it big as a songwriter in southern California.

Back in Pennsylvania after the war, Troup and his

Motor lodges in New Mexico and Missouri

Bobby Troup waves from the back seat of a 1948 Buick during a Salute to Route 66 parade in California in 1996.

wife, Cynthia, climbed into their stylish Buick convertible and struck out to make their fortunes. In Chicago they picked up Route 66 and headed west. As soon as they hit warm weather, they took down the car's canvas top and with the radio blaring, whizzed along, dreaming of their new life.

Somewhere during the trip, Cynthia suggested that her husband write a song about the highway they were traveling, Route 66. Bobby thought this was a swell idea. He started noodling around with words and a tune, using the names of some of the towns along the route, like Joplin, Missouri; Kingman, Barstow, and San Bernardino. By the time they reached Hollywood, the car had used 75 quarts of oil, and Troup had "Get Your Kicks on Route 66" half-written! Nat King Cole, one of the most popular singers of the time, recorded the song, which became a megahit. This catchy tune was a musical road map, mirroring the experiences of people of that era who were pulling up stakes to find a brighter future along Route 66.

The Mother Road was crowded with tourists, and the heavy military equipment of war-time convoys had chewed it up and left many stretches in sorry condition. To familiarize tourists with road conditions, Jack Rittenhouse wrote *A Guide Book to Highway 66* in 1946. This one-dollar book became the road bible for travelers of the time. The author not only listed the best lodgings, cafes, and tourist attractions but also offered handy tips and advice about the more than 2,000 miles of road:

"The entire highway from Chicago . . . is paved and passable," he said. "War-torn stretches of pavement are being repaired wherever pitted. Snow comes early and lingers late in stretches between Amarillo, Texas, and Kingman, Arizona, so inquire about road conditions ahead from gas stations when driving during November through March . . . . One of those war-surplus foxhole shovels takes little space and may come in very handy. . . .

"Carry a container of drinking water, which becomes a vital necessity as you enter the deserts. For chilly nights and early mornings, you'll find a camp blanket or auto robe useful—and it comes in handy if you find inadequate bedding in a tourist cabin."

Route 66 was booming. People were going west in private and public vehicles, and on top of almost anything that had wheels. They were looking for fun and adventure in the western United States.

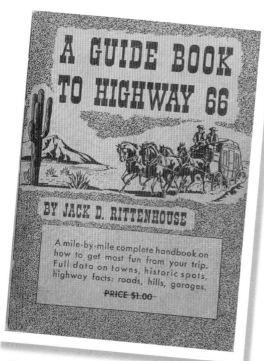

The guide book followed the road from east to west. If you were driving west to east, you simply started at the back of the book.

CHAPTER **FIVE**

"Let's stop at the
Jackalope place, Mother.
Please, please, please."

Martha Webb, age 8

ROADSIDE ATTRACTIONS

As Michael Wallis writes of the attractions of this cross-country artery in his book *Route 66: The Mother Road*, "Families could leave their homes…and drive out to the Grand Canyon or Painted Desert. They could go all the way to the Pacific on a highway that passed through towns where Abe Lincoln practiced law, Jesse James robbed banks, and Will Rogers learned to twirl a rope…cross Mark Twain's great river into land where outlaws hid in dark caves, and drive through picture-book countrysides where cowpokes still chased dogies into the sunset."

In those days, even signs alongside the road were fun to read, especially the Burma-Shave™ signs. These catchy little verses began popping up along the roadside in the fall of 1925. The first ones were placed around Minneapolis, Minnesota, but they soon blanketed highways from California to New York.

A series of Burma Shave™ signs as seen from inside a car in 1947

Everybody loved the corny little verses, split onto six narrow signs, that went something like this:

DON'T LOSE YOUR HEAD	THE WOLF	I'D HEARD IT PRAISED
TO SAVE A MINUTE	IS SHAVED	BY DRUGSTORE CLERKS
YOU NEED YOUR HEAD	SO NEAT AND TRIM	I TRIED THE STUFF
YOUR BRAINS	RED RIDING HOOD	HOT DOG!
ARE IN IT	IS CHASING HIM	IT WORKS!
BURMA-SHAVE	BURMA-SHAVE	BURMA-SHAVE

Motorists didn't read only the signs on their side of the highway. A passenger in the automobile was usually assigned to turn around backward, read the signs going in the opposite direction, and call out the words. Then everybody would attempt to unscramble the verses.

Businesses lining Route 66 did everything they could to grab the business of passing motorists. Some of the most colorful tourist attractions were the Indian trading posts of the Southwest. The famed Jack Rabbit Trading Post was one of the best-known because of its advertising. Bright yellow jack rabbit signs were plastered every few miles along the route.

After reading signs touting the trading post for hundreds of miles, vacationers were eager to stop when they finally arrived at the sprawling building topped with the same oversized

Jack Rabbit Trading Post in Joseph City, Arizona

A sign announcing the long-awaited Jack Rabbit Trading Post

yellow jack rabbit they had seen for miles. In front of the building, a large billboard showing the jack rabbit announced, HERE IT IS.

Inside, the trading post was stuffed with merchandise. Valuable Indian turquoise and silver jewelry was for sale, as were Indian rugs and blankets, leather purses and belts, and "genuine leather Indian moccasins." There were also inexpensive souvenirs and toys, such as wooden rattlesnakes, bows and arrows, lassos, firecrackers, inexpensive cowgirl and cowboy clothes, toy guns and holsters, pennants, and key chains.

Brightly colored postcards were best-selling items. Probably the card bought by most kids, as well as adults, pictured a jackalope. This mythical creature was part jack rabbit and part antelope. It had antlers and, according to legend, sang in a high human voice to soothe range cattle when the moon was full. Kids watched from the back seat as they rode along 66, hoping to see one loping across the desert. After dark they rolled down the car windows, straining to hear one of the animals crooning to cattle alongside the road. Nobody ever saw or heard one though.

To attract more business, some trading posts hired Native Americans to stage authentic dances for tourists. This turned out to be

Two jackalopes scan the horizon for cattle—or maybe gullible tourists!

CHAPTER SIX

great fun for the visitors but not so good for business, for when the dancers finished, travelers would pile back into their cars and continue on their way without doing any shopping. A more successful idea had native craftspeople demonstrating their leather or jewelry work on site. Tourists were eager to buy the items they had actually seen the tribal members create.

Rock shops are popular roadside attractions in Arizona

I Will Not Frighten My Mother

Bill Lucas remembers having to write 350 times, "I will never frighten my mother again" during a vacation trip from his home in Texas to Los Angeles. Why? The family had stopped at an Indian trading post somewhere in Arizona. The rest of the family sat having sodas at the fountain, but Bill slipped over to a counter and secretly bought a realistic wooden rattlesnake. He hurried out to the car before the rest had finished their drinks, coiled the toy serpent, and set it on the floor on the passenger side of the front seat, where his mother would be riding. The trick was a big success, he later reported. His mom screamed, danced around the car, and nearly had hysterics. The trick was not worth the price he paid though. He not only had to do all that writing but was also forbidden to enter another souvenir store for the rest of the trip.

Sometimes it seemed that the more outrageous the attraction, the more people stopped to gawk. Some of the most popular were the roadside animal and reptile farms featuring sluggish alligators lying like logs in huge water tanks, tame dancing bears on chains, caged panthers, and other wildlife. One place even advertised a two-headed calf! In one of these freakish places in New Mexico, a 15-foot king cobra and a 200-pound python were the stars of a mass of reptiles from India, Sumatra, and Malaysia. In addition, a Gila monster, a green mamba, and

46

a pit of writing rattlesnakes gave travelers plenty of thrills and chills. Some adults left these reptile farms shuddering and watching the ground, stepping high and checking their packages if anything moved or rattled. More than one fun-loving kid got into trouble for scaring the grownups with toy snakes they had surreptitiously bought and smuggled into the car before leaving the post.

The Blue Whale of Catoosa, Oklahoma, was once part of a water park on Route 66.

And when families were tired of sightseeing, where did they eat? In *Route 66 Remembered*, author Michael Witzel writes, "Whether it was Bob's Grill, Alice's Restaurant, Rosie's Diner, or Cathy's Cafe, most roadside dining spots had one thing in common— great customer service. In the days before the impersonal attitudes of today's fast-food restaurants were accepted as normal, friendly waitresses, talkative fry cooks, and helpful busboys made dining along the highway a real treat."

There were no fast-food establishments. For motorists in a hurry, there were drive-in cafes that provided curb service, where motorists could eat in their cars and then be on their way without delay. When an automobile pulled into the parking lot of a drive-in, a "carhop" hurried out with a menu to take orders.

In some drive-ins, these carhops, clad in satin uniforms, rolled out on skates. Travelers were often amazed to see slender girls carrying heavy trays stacked high with sizzling hamburgers, BLTs, hot dogs, club sandwiches, ice-cold root beers, and thick milkshakes without

Candy Made With Beans?

Moriarty, New Mexico, a small town on Route 66, is known as the Pinto Bean Capital of the World. For about 20 years, they've held a Pinto Bean Fiesta, and one of its most popular features is the Pinto Bean Cook-off. The following weird but tasty recipe won first prize in the Specialty Division in 1991.

<u>Terry Genger's Pinto Bean Fiesta Fudge</u>

1 cup warm cooked pinto beans

3/4 cup melted butter

1 cup cocoa

1 tablespoon vanilla

2 pounds powdered sugar

1 cup chopped pecans

Mash or sieve beans. Add melted butter, cocoa, and vanilla. Gradually stir in powdered sugar. Add nuts. Press all into 12 x 12-inch buttered pan. Store in refrigerator until ready to serve.

spilling a drop or falling down. And they did it on roller skates! When the food was ready, the carhop skated up to the vehicle with the loaded tray and clipped it onto the driver's window. After eating, the driver blinked the lights to signal the desire to leave. The carhops, who kept a sharp eye on all their customers, glided over, presented a bill, and removed the tray. In a moment, the motorists were on their way.

Root beer, a burger, and fries delivered on skates

Since Route 66 ran down the main streets of towns from Chicago to Los Angeles, travelers often enjoyed eating the "special of the day" at home-town cafes. It might be pot roast, or chicken dinner with hot biscuits and gravy, always with a generous slab of homemade pie. Most local folks were

The Texas Longhorn Motel provided everything travelers needed—good food, friendly service, gasoline, and a place to spend the night.

The beautiful Blue Swallow Motel in Tucumcari, New Mexico, was built in 1939.

Restroom Inspections

The Phillips Petroleum service stations hired six registered nurses togged out in spiffy uniforms to inspect their restrooms to be sure they were sanitary. All day these "highway hostesses" cruised the length of 66, making sure the Phillips stations were as clean as advertised. If the station restrooms did not pass inspection, the hostesses reported the failure to the head office in Bartlesville, Oklahoma, and the station manager was ordered to scrub the facilities until they were clean.

friendly to travelers and enjoyed hearing about other parts of the country. Before television, people from, say, Texas, knew little about the Midwest or states like New Jersey or Rhode Island. To meet somebody from New York City was a thrill for them.

As travel increased, motels became all the rage. The new word *motel* combined the words *motor* and *hotel*. Competition was stiff as owners vied for business. They designed their lodgings to be as eye-catching as possible, erecting huge neon signs to grab the attention of passing motorists.

Even in the Midwest, a western theme was the most popular motel design along Route 66. Flashing neon signs featured cowboys in Stetsons, boots, and spurs. Snorting stallions with flaring nostrils and Indian chiefs in feathered headdresses were also neon favorites.

Since an Indian theme was often used in businesses along Route 66, it was not long before someone built a motel with units shaped like wigwams. That man was Frank Redford, from Horse Cave, Kentucky. He got the notion on a trip to California when he ate in a cafe in Long Beach that was shaped like a wigwam. When he returned home, he opened his own wigwam restaurant. It was an instant hit, so he added a motel with wigwam units near the restaurant. The combination restaurant and motel was so successful that he built others along Route 66 and elsewhere. Redford boasted that the lunchroom was the largest wigwam in the world, containing 13 tons of steel and 38 tons of concrete.

Excitement ran high when the family sedan exited the highway into the parking lot. Everybody wanted to spend at least one night in a wigwam. (Although we would take a dim view of such ideas today, these businesses were never intended to be demeaning or insulting to Native Americans.)

One of Frank Redford's seven wigwam villages as seen on an old postcard

Other novelty lodgings were train motels. These started as a way of using whatever buildings or materials were available for the housing of travelers. One such train establishment in Texas was called the Hobo Motel and consisted of 11 boxcars that had been converted into 12 x 18-foot rooms. The caboose housed a lounge and lobby for patrons. Spending the night in a boxcar, caboose, or a Pullman car intrigued many travelers. Sometimes families had to draw straws to see who would sleep in the upper berths.

CHAPTER SIX

Train-car motels such as this one in Washington
(not on Route 66) were popular novelty lodging spots.

By 1960, Route 66 was being replaced by interstate highways, but anyone with a TV could pretend to travel the road right from home. A popular CBS television series, *Route 66*, about two young characters named Buz Murdock and Tod Stiles, was a favorite show across the United States. Every Friday night until the hour-long show went off the air in 1964, thousands of families watched as Buz and Tod cruised 66 and environs in a shiny Corvette, looking for adventure. But like that TV show, the days of the great road were numbered.

Buz Murdock (George Maharis) and Tod Stiles (Martin Milner) and their Corvette, ready to roll on Route 66

53

I wanted to drive the
American roads at the
century's end, to look
at the country again,
from border to border
and beach to beach.

Larry McMurtry

Chapter Seven

THE DEATH OF THE ROAD

Although Route 66 had a few four-lane divided stretches, it was basically a narrow, two-lane road. By the 1950s, it could barely handle the large volume of automobile traffic. It was so dangerous that folks called it "Bloody 66" because of the many automobile accidents that occurred there. One section in the Ozark Mountains was known as the Devil's Elbow because of its dangerous curves and turns.

A woman who traveled this road as a child remembers that her father grew so nervous when they reached this part of Route 66 that "my sister and I got deathly still and sat without talking" as her father navigated the twisting highway. "He gripped the steering wheel so tightly that his knuckles turned white," she said. Although most people drove sensibly, there were others who did not slow down on the curves and blind corners, and it was then that tragedy occurred.

In Arizona the most dangerous portions of the road were called Camino de la Muerte (Highway of Death), where head-on crashes happened again and again. In 1956, it was reported that one of every six traffic deaths in Arizona occurred on Route 66. Small white wooden crosses were placed alongside the road in spots where people had perished in traffic accidents in hopes that these grim reminders would slow speeding drivers. It probably helped, but accidents continued, as high-speed automobiles raced along a highway that had been designed for much slower vehicles.

Large trucks also added to the perils of traveling the two-lane sections of Route 66. From the earliest days of the road, it had been a favorite for long-distance hauling. Not only was it a shorter route from Chicago to California, but it also passed through a milder climate than northern highways, making it even more attractive to truckers. By the 1930s, Route 66 was crowded with large vehicles highballing across the country. The road was widened and straightened in places, but there were just too many vehicles on the highway. The sight of a pair of huge trucks squeezing past each other on the narrow road was terrifying. Finally traffic grew so heavy that four-lane, limited-access highways across the nation became a necessity.

In 1954, President Dwight D. Eisenhower appointed a President's Advisory Committee on a National Highway Program to investigate the situation. Eisenhower had traveled Route 66 as an army officer in World War II and had even then realized its drawbacks as he tried to keep people and supplies moving. Then, while he was Supreme Commander of the Allied Forces, he had traveled the German autobahn (high-speed limited-access highway) and came to appreciate it. As a result of his encouragement and the studies made by his advisory committee, Congress established the Federal-Aid Highway Act of 1956, which set forth guidelines for a 42,500-mile (68,395 km) national interstate highway system.

CHAPTER SEVEN

The interstate highways came slowly, however—a piece of road here, a few miles there, with bypasses constructed around cities in several states. It had taken about 12 years to pave the length of Route 66 the first time; now it would take twice that long to replace it with four-lane interstate highways.

The U.S. Highway 66 Association fought hard to prevent the destruction of America's Main Street. Cy Avery and Lon Scott, the men who had worked hard to bring the road into being, protested, but they were elderly now and powerless to save America's Main Street. The last stretch was replaced in 1984. Once more, tumbleweed scratched across the desert, whipped into fences, and piled up on the empty road. Coyotes loped along the pavement that had once been the busiest highway in the United States.

It wasn't all that easy to replace the Mother Road. It took five different interstate highways: Interstate 55 from Chicago, Illinois, to St. Louis, Missouri; Interstate 44 from St. Louis to Oklahoma City, Oklahoma; Interstate 40 from Oklahoma City to Barstow, California; Interstate 15 from Barstow to San Bernardino, California; and Interstate 10 from San Bernardino to Santa Monica, California.

The loss of Route 66 drained the life from most of the small towns that had been in its path. They were left as shadows of the bustling communities they had once been. Even towns along the new superslab's path were isolated by high chain-link fences and the lack of exit ramps. In some ways it seemed that the interstates that linked one side of the United States with the other had simultaneously split the country.

Route 66 Elementary School

On September 19, 1998, Edgewood, New Mexico, celebrated the opening of the Route 66 Elementary School. Situated near the remains of the Mother Road, the outside of the school building features a colorful red, white, and turquoise emblem with black 66 lettering. Inside the school, students can travel from Chicago, Illinois, at the school's main entrance, past the Route 66 library, and on to Santa Monica, California. The walls of the school picture the maps of the states through which the road passed. The halls are painted with a double stripe down the middle, like a highway. Students always walk on the right side of the hallway.

ROUTE 66 MAIN STREET OF AMERICA

Abandoned gas station along Route 66 in Arizona in 1991

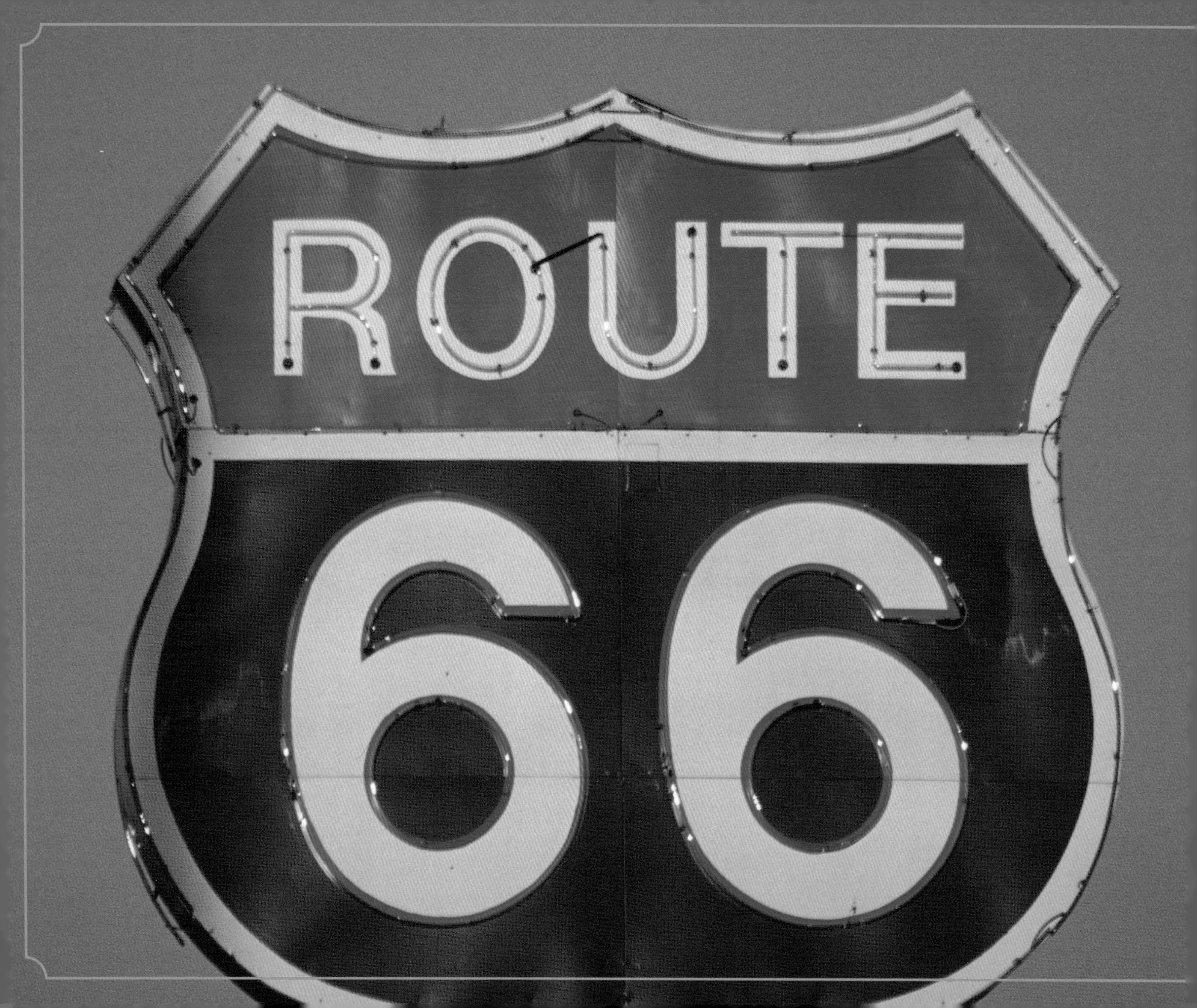
ROUTE
66

When the final strip of Route 66, near Williams, Arizona, was abandoned, the road was replaced by a portion of Interstate 40. A grand celebration was held, with speeches by highway dignitaries and much hoopla. Even Bobby Troup took part in the celebration. But some people felt that it was more like a funeral for a dear old friend.

And so Route 66 became a ghost road. Although interstate highways were considered "progress," not everyone thought it was all that great to be able to drive from Chicago to Santa Monica without stopping. Many travelers missed rambling along, stopping at small-town cafes, eating homemade pie, and talking to the friendly waitress who served it. They missed the small motels and funky businesses that had enabled them to break up their journeys in the past. They missed the feeling of being connected to people in towns across the United States. Traveling the mighty interstates could be pretty monotonous. Motorists missed getting their "kicks on Route 66," when getting there was definitely half the fun.

Route 66 Timeline

1920

Cyrus Avery spearheads the effort to join Chicago, Illinois, and Los Angeles, California, passing the highway through his hometown of Tulsa, Oklahoma.

1921

Federal-Aid Highway Act is passed, creating a system of interconnected interstate highways.

1925

Avery works with the committee appointed to join hundreds of roads already in use into the system that would become Route 66.

1926

Federal-Aid Highway Act requires the government to channel significant funding toward the maintenance and improvement of a highway linking the East to the West.

Route 66 is officially commissioned from Chicago to Los Angeles (2,448 miles of roadway) on November 11. Only 800 of those miles are paved; the rest are some form of dirt or gravel.

1927

The U.S. 66 Highway Association is established to expedite the building of the highway.

The nickname "Main Street of America" is adopted.

Phillips 66 adopts the number and logo, and new gas stations appear along the highway.

1928

The First Annual International Trans-Continental Foot Race, or "Bunion Derby," begins in Los Angeles on March 4. The race is won by Andy Payne, who ran the 3,422.3 miles in 84 days in 573 hours, 4 minutes, and 34 seconds.

1929

A report shows the route fully paved in Kansas and Illinois, 66% paved in Missouri, and 25% improved in Oklahoma. The 1,200 mile western section (except California's metropolitan areas) were not paved. Texas, New Mexico, Arizona, and parts of southeastern California totaled only 64 miles of paved highway along Route 66 until the height of the Depression.

1931

On January 5, Missouri is the third state to pave its whole section of Route 66. Workmen throw coins into the wet pavement to celebrate.

1933

The U.S. government hires thousands of unemployed young men to work on road gangs to pave the remaining sections of Route 66.

1934-1936

Dust storms and drought drive thousands of people from their homes, mostly fleeing west along Route 66. An estimated 210,000 people migrate to California to find a better life.

1935

Route 66 is extended from Los Angeles to its end point in Santa Monica, California, on June 17.

Also on that day, Route 66 is rerouted over the Chain of Rocks Bridge in St. Louis, Missouri.

1937

Route 66's original path changes in New Mexico, where its original 506 miles become only 399 miles. On September 26, Route 66 is moved west from Santa Rosa to Albuquerque, bypassing Santa Fe.

1938

The last unpaved section of Route 66, in Oldham County, Texas, is paved.

Route 66 Timeline

1939

The Grapes of Wrath by John Steinbeck is published, in which Route 66 is named "the Mother Road, the road of flight" by the author.

Graham Greene coins the term *tourist trap*, possibly in relation to Route 66.

1940

The Grapes of Wrath is made into a movie, which makes Route 66 famous in the annals of American lore.

1941

The United States enters World War II.

1942

Because of the war, auto production ends, gasoline rationing begins, and tires are hard to get—all of which negatively impact Route 66.

1945

World War II ends, and many Americans begin recreational traveling.

1946

Jack D. Rittenhouse publishes *A Guide Book to Highway 66*, which lists every town along the highway, as well as attractions, services, and places to stay.

Bobby Troup, writes "Get Your Kicks on Route 66." The popular recording is released by singer Nat King Cole.

1950s

Route 66 itself becomes a destination. Tourist traps become common as well.

1953

Turner Turnpike (I-44) between Tulsa and Oklahoma City, Oklahoma, opens, bypassing 100 miles of Route 66 and the first blow to its immortality is dealt. The federal government's 4-lane interstate system replaces section after section in other states.

1957

President Eisenhower sets up the National Interstate Highway System, to be completed by 1972. It was finalized in 1982.

1960

Route 66 TV series, starring Martin Milner and George Maharis, debuts on October 7. The show ran 116 episodes and closed on September 18, 1964.

1962

States' petition to have the interstates renumbered as I-66 from Chicago to Los Angeles is, not surprisingly, refused.

1970

Nearly all of the original Route 66 is now bypassed by a 4-lane highway.

1977

Route 66 is decommissioned in Illinois.

1984

Final section of the Mother Road is bypassed by Interstate 40 at Williams, Arizona, on October 13.

1985

Route 66 is officially decommissioned, and its highway markers are removed.

1999

Congress passes an act to create the Route 66 Corridor Preservation Program, administered by the National Park Service. Private property owners; nonprofit organizations; and local, state, federal, and tribal governments collaborate on Route 66 preservation issues.

BIBLIOGRAPHY

CLARK, MARIAN, *The Route 66 Cookbook*, Council Oaks Books, 2000.

KELLY, SUSAN CROCE AND SCOTT, QUINTA, *Route 66: The Highway and Its People*,

  University of Oklahoma Press, 1988.

REPP, THOMAS, *Route 66: The Empires of Amusement*, Mock Turtle Press, 1999.

RITTENHOUSE, JACK D., *A Guide Book to Highway 66*. 1946.

  Facsimile © 1989 by Univ. of New Mexico Press.

SNYDER, TOM, *The Route 66: Traveler's Guide and Roadside Companion*, St. Martin's Press, 1990.

STEINBECK, JOHN, *The Grapes of Wrath*, Viking Press, 1939.

WALLIS, MICHAEL, *Route 66: The Mother Road*, St. Martin's Press, 2001.

WITZEL, MICHAEL, *Route 66 Remembered*, Motorbooks International, 1996.

WEBSITES

www.national66.com

NATIONAL HISTORIC ROUTE 66 FEDERATION

The nonprofit organization dedicated to
preserving Route 66 across the country

www.oklahomaroute66.com

Oklahoma Route 66 Association

www.missouri66.org

Route 66 Association of Missouri

www.rt66nm.org

New Mexico Route 66 Association

www.azrt66.com

Historic Route 66 Association of Arizona

www.il66assoc.org

Route 66 Association of Illinois

www.barbwiremuseum.com/TexasRoute66.htm

Texas Old Route 66 Association

INDEX